A Comprehensive Beginners Guide To Successful Investing

By Rodney Wall

Table of Contents

Table of Contents

Introduction

All adults must learn how to invest their money. Unfortunately, this topic is not taught in our basic education systems. Most people never learn the proper way of investing. They don't invest because they don't want to risk their money in something that they do not understand.

This book aims to change all that. It contains the essential information to understand the concepts of stocks, bonds and other popular investing vehicles. Regardless of your appetite for risk, there is a suitable investing vehicle for you. This book aims to guide you to find the best one.

It also teaches you the strategies and the best practices in investing in these investment vehicles. Aside from this, the book also includes a guide on how to get started.

Thanks again for downloading this book, I hope you enjoy it!

Chapter 1 – Fundamentals of Investing

Many people want to start investing but they do not know how to. Most courses and books about it are expensive and full of finance jargons. Because of lack of knowledge, the aspiring investors who read these books either lose interest in investing, or start their investing experience badly.

In this chapter, we will discuss the basics of investing. By learning these details, you will know how to separate good investments from bad ones. You will also know what investing is and what mindsets are needed to start doing it.

Investing in a nutshell

Investing refers to a variety of business activities where in the investor spends money with the intent to gain profits. The investment scheme should increase the value of the money invested through legitimate business activities.

In its most basic sense, investing refers to the act of spending money to fund a business. For example, your friend John wants to open a small gym in the neighborhood. However, he does not have enough capital to start the business. He asks you if you want to invest in his business.

Having seen that many people are interested in joining John's future gym, you gave him $50,000 or half of what he needs to start. John agrees that you will get half of the net income of the business.

John used the funds to make his gym presentable and added a few more workout tools. The business became a success. In the first six months, John's gym gained enough members to cover the capital.

By the end of the sixth month, John calculated the average income of the gym at $10,000 per month. A fourth of this amount is used for the bills of the gym. A fourth of the income is reinvested back to the business. The last quarter of the income is divided by the partners, you and John.

John gave you $2,500 every month as part of your share of the profit. By the 20th month, the income from the business already paid off the initial amount you invested. Any amount you receive after that is purely profit from your investment.

While this example led to a positive outcome, sometimes, businesses could go south. Whenever you invest your money, you expose it to risks that may decrease the value of your investment. If John's gym for example, had a competitor that took all his members, he will not be able to make profits. In the process, he will fail to pay you back. It would take a lot longer to regain your money back.

Here are some other negative effects of investing your money:

You risk losing it when businesses go bankrupt

When a business fails to make money, it uses up its resources with nothing to show for it. Part of the resources that it uses up is the money of the investors. If the business does not adapt to market conditions, it will go bankrupt. Investors don't get their money back in this situation.

You lose liquidity of your money

In the finance world, liquid assets refer to cash. When you put your money in an investment, it becomes difficult to convert the money back to cash. If you need the money immediately, your invested amount may lose some of its value in the process of converting it back to cash.

When you buy a brand new car for example, it decreases in value every day that you use it. If you need to sell your car because of an emergency, you may have trouble looking for buyers. Because of this, you would be forced to sell the car at a lower price than you purchased it. Smart investors never consider buying a brand new car as an investment.

You subject your money to risks that are outside of your control

Your invested funds may also lose their value due to factors outside of your control. Market and political conditions, for instance, often make a negative impact in the stock market.

Let's say you invested in a company that manufactures smartphones. Today, the company does very well because of the popularity of their product. Let's say for example that a week from now, another company launches a product that effectively replaces smartphones as the primary communication device.

The company you invested in will have trouble selling their products. The products that they already have in stock will not move as fast as they expected. Because of this, the value of the company decreases. If you liquidate (turn your shares of the company into cash by selling it) your assets at this point, the value of your investment will go down.

There is no way for a casual investor to know about such market factors in advance. Even if you are diligent in studying the market and its major players, you can still be blindsided by factors that are not mentioned in the media or investment researchers.

When investing, your goal is to put your money in an investment vehicle with the highest potential of returns. However, you also need to minimize the risks that come with investing. You can do this by following these tips:

Learn before you invest

Most of the people who lose money while investing do not learn about the business or the market where they invest. Investors need to learn how the companies they invest in make money. They should also consider the potential for growth of these companies.

If you were the investor, consider the market factors that affect that company. This includes risks that affect the entire sector where that company belongs. If you invested in a company that produces cars, for example, you should at least learn about the competition of that company in its industry.

You should consider the economy-wide factors that may affect your investment. While these factors are usually out of your control, learning about them will help you anticipate. You will be able to see warning signs for market bubbles and the risk of a recession. Most importantly, you could react to these warning signs to protect your investment from incurring losses.

All these will be discussed in future chapters.

Diversify your assets

If you have $100,000 and you want to invest it, don't spend it all in one company stock. If the company goes bankrupt, you will lose your entire invested amount. Instead, look for different investment vehicles so that your money is not exposed to one particular type of risk. You could invest half of it in stocks and the other half divided between bonds, low-cost index funds and Government treasury bills. The amount invested in stocks should also be divided into multiple companies and sectors.

Keep important funds out of risk

While it may be tempting to invest all your money in one sure investment opportunity, don't do it. Keep the money for important things like your child's college fund out of risk. Place your healthcare, educational and retirement funds in low-risk types of investment vehicles. Your retirement fund for example, should be placed in the 401(k) fund offered by your company.

Build an emergency fund

Keep an emergency fund for unexpected life events. If you lose your job for instance, having an emergency fund allows you to avoid touching your invested amounts. Keep an emergency fund 3-5 times the size of your monthly income. If you are unable to work for some reason, you have 3-5 months to recover and find a job.

Build a network of investing friends

Make it a habit to talk to experts about investing. Find people in your circles who also invest. Ask them of their preferred investment strategies and the investment vehicles they take part in. You will learn a lot more from experiences of other people than you ever will from books.

You could use the information you gain from other successful investors. You could replicate their actions to achieve similar results. By also learning about people's mistakes, you will be able to avoid doing them when it is your time to invest.

Savings and investment before lifestyle expenses

People often fail to invest because they do not have a saving system. As a result, they spend all their income on lifestyle expenses. Some of them even forget about where they spent their money.

To avoid this from happening, you need a simple system for investing. One way to do it is by setting your money aside and investing it before you start spending for lifestyle expenses. When your income arrives, save a percentage of it and put it in a savings account. You park your money in the savings account until you find a good time to invest it.

Ideally the savings account should not be easily accessible. Keep its ATM card safe at home. Don't bring it with you when you go shopping or when you go out with your friends. Only take money from it if it's the right time to invest.

Chapter 2 – Learning about Investment Markets

Now that we know the potential risks and advantages of investing, let's discuss how you can start investing. In our example above, you and John, the gym owner, are already friends. Let's say you don't know anyone who wants to start a business. How will you start investing?

The Investment Markets

You have a $100,000 that you want to set aside for at least five years. You want to invest it but you don't know anyone who wants to start a business.

This is where the investment market comes in. Investment markets are platforms where investors can find investment opportunities. In general, a market is a place where buyers and sellers meet. In an investment market, the investors usually start as the buyers.

They buy investment assets from the previous owners. Assets refer to publicly traded, tangible or intangible properties. These properties each have value, which is stated in a contract. In investing, assets fall in three main categories, equities, fixed income and cash equivalents. Each one will be discussed in future chapters.

The previous owners of the assets could be companies that need money for business growth or other investors who need to turn their assets into cash.

The stock market is one of the best examples of an investment market. In this type of market, people are buying and selling shares (units of ownership) of a company.

The assets bought and sold in a market are usually priced based on market conditions. The law of supply and demand applies in the pricing of these assets. If there are many people selling their shares of a company, this will generally drive the price down. The price goes down because there is an increased supply of that specific asset in the market.

The price is balanced by the number of investors who want to own shares of that company. Because there are many people who want to own these assets, the demand for it increases. This drives prices of that specific asset up.

Market factors

As stated in the previous chapter, there are certain factors that affect the market as a whole. These factors affect the balance of supply and demand in the market. Here are some of them:

People's impression of the market

Most people love the idea of making their money grow. However, many beginners do not do enough research about the market before they start investing. Many first-time investors are talked into investing when the market is booming.

People see in the news that the market is doing well and they want to take advantage of the booming economy. Because many people want to buy assets from the market, the demand in the market increases. This also drives prices up.

In the opposite end of the spectrum, people's impression of the market conditions could also drive prices down. The most obvious example of such an event is the bursting of an economic bubble.

The 2000 Tech Bubble

In the years prior to the year 2000, internet businesses were booming. This was the time when companies like eBay and Amazon started becoming popular. Both companies were only 4-6 years old but they were already getting a lot of attention.

Because of the popularity of these companies and others like them, other business people started building online businesses. Investors funded many of these companies in the hopes that they will become part owner of the future tech giants for a small price.

This drove investors to buy companies with no track record. The hype in the market also invited small time and beginner investors. Many beginners bought stocks of companies they just heard about. Without proper research, these small time investors were practically gambling their money on untested companies with no track record.

Most of the companies at the time did not have solid business plans and proven products or services. These companies burned through their capital without showing profit. However, the demand in the market kept driving the prices of these tech companies up. Because many of these companies do not have profitable products or services, many of them failed.

The first people who realized that there was a market bubble were able to gain profit by liquidating their profits early. The massive sell-off of some of the major players prompted other players to also pull their money out. One by one, each poorly performing tech company fell.

The biggest losers are the people who bought their shares late and those who failed to sell their assets in time. The majority of these losers were small time and beginner investors who were caught up in the hype of the market.

In the years that followed, beginners were wary of investing in the stock market. The media was filled with stories about people who lost everything in the economic crisis. Beginner investors did not want to take part in investing in the stock market because of the gloomy picture that the media paints.

Because of people's negative view of the market, stock prices were generally low after the crash.

Government activities

The government of each country also has a big role to play in their corresponding investment markets. In the US government for example, it is the central government's role to decrease unemployment. To deal with this perpetually growing concern, the central government funds projects and encourages businesses to grow. When the central government performs well in this aspect of its job, the economy generally improves, businesses grow, jobs are created and people have more money to spend.

However, human nature sometimes pushes growth too far. Business owners and investors generally want to compete in the market. They want to get the largest part of the market share in their respective industries. Apple for example, wants everyone to buy phones from them. Microsoft on the other hand, wants everybody to use their operating system. Every business in America wants better profits compared to what they earned the previous year.

To cope with the unrealistic demands of investors, businesses sometimes need to borrow money from banks and other big financial institutions. Borrowing money boosts the activity of a business. It allows them to grow even though they don't have liquid assets at the moment.

Banks and financial institutions do not mind letting big businesses borrow money because most of them have good track records for paying debt. Even if they fail in their business endeavors, these big businesses could still repay their debts by liquidating some of their assets.

Smaller businesses, on the other hand, usually have a harder time getting loans. Lenders don't like lending them money because they are more likely to go bankrupt. Most small business owners do not have enough credit history to justify big debts.

However, banks and lending institutions also wants to make money. Their primary way of making profits is through interest payments of debtors. Some lenders allow less reliable businesses to borrow money in exchange for high interest rates. If unchecked, the excessive borrowing of businesses can lead to a debt crisis.

In an attempt to lessen the lending activities of debtors in an impending debt crisis, the central bank interferes by adjusting their own interest rates. When the central bank increases the interest rates for example, people do not want to borrow because the cost of borrowing is too expensive. When this happens, businesses look for other means to fund their business endeavors. At the same time, the growth of debt in the economy slows down.

When the central bank does this, investor activities are usually influenced. In the US for example, the long awaited interest rates increase boosts the demand of debt instrument markets like bonds. In the process, it may slow down the activity in equity markets around the world. This will result to increase in bond prices and a general decrease in stock prices.

Economic conditions of big economies

When giant economies fail, all investors around the world hold their breath to see what will happen next. When economies of the US and China go down, the economies all countries trading with them are affected. These two nations are the biggest importers of goods and services because they have a massive market to satisfy. When these countries experience a crisis, the spending power of their people is also affected. Their citizens do not want to spend money because of the economic crisis.

Let's say, China's economy slowed down and its stock market took a dive. In general, the value of the assets of its citizens decreases. Some of these assets are for retirement. To make sure that they still have enough money for retirement, most people in China will allocate more of their income into their retirement and savings fund.

As a result, they will spend less on expensive items like the products imported from the US. Some industries in the US will be affected. The lower sales volume of these companies will be reflected in their stock prices in the future.

Political changes in big economies

Changing of the guard in politics could create fluctuations in the market prices of securities. If the investors generally like the new president for example, there may be stability or even an increase in the stock prices. People want to buy more stocks because they feel that the new president will improve economic situations in the years to come.

However, if investors do not like the new president, there may be massive selling of stocks that leads to a decrease in stock prices. This happens because of uncertainties in the market.

If the policies promised by the new president will create changes in the market, there may be a decrease in stock prices in the future. This makes people want to sell now, when the prices are still high.

Two Types of Market Conditions: The Bear and the Bull

Investors and the media in general describe markets as either bearish or bullish. Bearish markets refer to an economic environment where prices are going down. Some analysts suggest that a bearish market is confirmed when the general value of the market takes a 20% dive.

Let's say the stock market has been increasing in value for the last few years. This year, it peaked to 1,000 points. However, a series of political and economic events made the people wary in investing. The paranoid investors started selling their shares while they could still make profits.

The general market dropped from 1,000 points to 900 points in a week. At this point, the market is not yet bearish. Market values fluctuate at these levels all the time. However, if the market dips down to 800 points in the following week, analysts will now consider the market as bearish.

The bull market is the opposite. When the market value increases continuously, people call the market condition as bull market. This is the reason why they have a statue of the bull outside of New York Stock Exchange.

The bull market happens because of a demand in the market. This commonly happens when the economy is doing very well. For the market to become bullish, investors should have a positive outlook towards the government and the general economic conditions.

Chapter 3 – The Stock Market

The stock market is probably the most popular of all securities market because it has been the focal point of many Hollywood movies. The average Joe thinks that people who participate in the stock market are rich. They also think that one can win or lose big amounts in this market. Most people who are not well versed with investments think that investing in the stock market is like gambling.

Experienced investors think differently. They think of the stock market as an investment vehicle with high risk and high rewards potential. If you want to learn how to invest in the stock market, learn how it works first.

As of the writing of this book, the total market capitalization of the world market amount to more than $70 trillion. As of 2012, the US has the largest market capitalization of all markets. It is followed by Japan and China.

Before we begin, let's first discuss a common cause of confusion in terminology used. In future discussions, we will be using the words stock and shares interchangeably. Both words mean the same. You could also call the stock market as the shares market. When reading other books, you will also see other financial gurus using the term 'equity' in the place of stocks or shares. This term is also acceptable.

How the stock market works

The stock market is a platform where shares of companies are bought and sold. Shares refer to units of ownership of a company listed in the stock exchange. When you buy company shares, the law considers you as one of the owners of that company. Just like all the other owners, you are entitled to a part of the assets and future profits of the company. If the company grows, the value of your share also grows.

Each share you own of a specific company represents a percentage of ownership. Let's say that Company X has one million total shares. The majority shareholders are the people directly involved in the business including the company executives. You are one of the top executives of this company and you own one hundred thousand shares of the company. This means that you own 10% of the company.

Investors however, do not aim to buy as many shares as possible. They prefer to buy the stocks with the best potential for growth. Because of this, they usually allocate their funds into many different companies.

Each shareholder has a right to vote for the members of the board of directors of the company. Because most investors have very small stakes in the companies they own, they rarely exercise this right.

When an investor buys shares, he should receive a stock certificate. In the past, these certificates were traded like real property. If you wanted to buy stocks in the past, you need to find someone with a stock certificate. When the company gives out dividends, they used to require each shareholder to present their stock certificates for them to receive their share.

Investors nowadays do not get a chance to see the stock certificate. In the place of the traditional certificates, the companies in the stock exchange and the brokers keep track of the changes of ownership of shares electronically. This makes the process of buying and selling shares much faster.

From an investor's point of view, the stock market is an opportunity to increase the value of their investment portfolio. For most investors, stocks are the centerpiece of their portfolio. They put the largest part of their investment fund in stocks to maximize profits.

You could also do the same. However, you first need to learn how you could actually earn money from the stock market.

What's in it for the company?

Most companies usually start as small business ideas implemented by a sole proprietor or a partnership. They are usually self-funded or funded through an angel investor. Eventually, the successful ones grow to become medium-sized enterprises.

Sometimes, the owner of the company has bigger dreams for his business. However, he doesn't have the funds to take it to the next level. This is why companies opt to list their businesses in the stock market. If the business is popular enough, it could do well in its Initial Public Offering (IPO) and collect enough funds to create a giant corporation.

Companies that list their business in the stock exchange do so for different reasons. The most common of which is to get more capital for business growth. By listing their company in the stock market, they get access to trillions of dollars' worth of investment funds. You can observe the capital gathering power of the stock market in the IPOs of popular companies.

Recent giant IPOs

When Facebook and Twitter first got listed in the stock exchange, people were so excited and the hype drove the prices of these IPOs beyond the ideal price. Facebook, for instance, raised around $16 billion of additional funding from their IPO alone.

With this privilege however, comes the responsibility of the company to its investors. It is the company's responsibility to increase its own value so that investors are rewarded. In the process, the company also ensures its survival by keeping itself actively growing.

This method of getting capital is beneficial to the business because the only other way to get this amount of money is through borrowing from banks.

Types of shares

Stocks come in two forms, common and preferred stocks.

Preferred stocks

This type of company stocks is not commonly traded in the market. It has some unique qualities that make owning it attractive to the investor. Its defining characteristic is that it usually comes with a guaranteed and fixed dividend. This guaranteed feature is not present in common stocks.

Preferred stockholders also get special treatment when the company is giving out money. When there is a general distribution of dividends for example, the preferred stockholders get their dividends first before everybody else.

When the company decides to end its operations and liquidate its assets, the preferred stock holders are paid first after all the financial liabilities of the company have been paid for.

Generally, preferred stocks are priced higher and most of them do not come with the usual right to vote. Since most investors do not exercise this right anyway, this disadvantage does not bother most people.

Common stocks

Common shares are the ones that are often traded in the market. It does not come with the special treatment given to preferred stocks. However, it does come with the right to vote for board of directors. For people inside the company, owning the most common stocks can be a source of power.

The real difference between the two

Looking at the features, most people would think that preferred stocks are always superior to common stocks. Each type of stocks has its own value. Most investors see preferred stocks as the less risky type of investment. The guaranteed dividends that come with most preferred stocks allow investors to start earning their money back even without liquidating their assets. If the company does not work out, the special treatment given to preferred stockholders could be an advantage because they are paid first before common stockholders.

While common stocks do not have these privileges, it also has its own appealing characteristics. One of which is its potential for massive capital appreciation. Historically, preferred stocks do not grow as fast in value as common stocks. The primary reason is because preferred stocks are priced higher from the start. It is also traded less often in the market. There is a lower demand for preferred stocks, slowing its growth in value down.

Its counterpart on the other hand, is frequently traded. If you observe both types of stocks, you will notice that the guaranteed dividends of preferred stocks usually take the lead early in the investment period. As time passes however, the prices of common stocks of good companies rise faster. The dividends in preferred stocks are usually fixed. The growth of your investment with preferred stocks is usually limited.

Another important difference between the two is that preferred stocks are 'callable'. The company could buy the preferred stocks back from you if they wish and you could do nothing about it. Because of this feature, people think of preferred stocks as not true units of ownership. Some investors even refer to them as debt instruments similar to bonds.

Two ways your investment grows in the stock market

Dividends

The total amount that the company gives out is divided by the total number of outstanding shares. Let's say a small company is giving out five million dollars in dividends. Their company is divided into ten million shares. If we divide the sum of money by the number of shares, we can assume that each share should get $0.50.

If you own 300 shares of this company, you could expect to get $150 in dividends. The more shares you own in that company, the bigger your dividend payment will be.

Some companies make it a tradition to reward their loyal investors. They do this by giving out dividends. Dividends refer to amounts of money or shares given out by the company to their investors. When a company has a strong performance in the previous year for example, they may use the excess of their profits as a way to thank their investors.

Not all companies however, give out dividends. In fact, most companies in the stock market choose not to do it. They choose to put their profits back in the company. They reinvest the money to make the company grow.

If you don't get dividends however, how will your investment grow?

Capital appreciation

You can still make your investment grow, even when investing in companies that do not give out dividends. Your investment grows through capital appreciation if you buy low and sell high. When the company makes profit and chooses to hold on to its profits, they usually reinvest the money to improve their business performance.

Companies, especially the big ones, are focused on growth. They want to keep growing at a faster pace. Even the ones that performed exceptionally well last year, wants to outdo their own record and grow at an even faster pace this year.

To keep their momentum going, these types of businesses need resources to fund their growth. Fast food brands for instance, need funds to build more stores. A local brand on the other hand, may need money to expand their operations in new markets.

Most of the time, businesses borrow money from banks or willing investors to fund their growth. However, these sources of funds come with a cost, the interest. When businesses borrow, they are sacrificing their future profits for faster growth.

When businesses use their own profits to fund their growth, they no longer need to worry about interest payments and sacrificing future profits. If the growth project is successful, the company's overall value will grow with no added costs. In theory, when the overall value of the company grows, so does the value of your shares.

In reality however, it is the market that determines the value of your company. The results of the business activities of the company should be observable to the people participating in the market. If people see improvements in the company's growth, more of them will want to buy the shares of the company. The increased demand of the shares of the company increases its price. If you sell your share at a point when the prices are high, then, you have made your investment grow through capital appreciations.

Let's say you bought 500 shares of Company Y, a car company, at $1 per share. You spent a total of $500. In the time that you hold their shares, Company Y has released two new car models that are selling fast. It is the most popular new model in the season. After a year of holding their shares, each share is now worth $1.25. Your $500 capital is now $625 if you decide to sell your shares now.

Types of players in the stock market

When participating in the stock market, you must understand that not everyone in there uses the same investment principle as you do. Some people are more aggressive in buying and selling stocks than others. By understanding how other people invest, you will be able to anticipate how the market in general will react to certain changes in economic conditions.

Long term investors

Some people and organizations, do not want to take risks in the market. They just buy relatively safe companies and let their investment grow for a long period. While this way of investing is not exciting, it is safer if you know how to pick the right companies.

When the market is down, these people do not even consider touching their investments. They know that all economic issues are temporary. The market always recovers even from the worst situations.

This type of investing is unpopular because most people want to see immediate progress from their investment activities.

Active investors

Active investors are more involved with the market. They have a combination of high and low risk stocks in their portfolio. Most of the younger active investors generally gravitate towards riskier stocks. They know that they can recover if they lose money in risky companies.

However, as active investors become older, they tend to reallocate their funds to safer companies. The ones who are in their forties and fifties are nearer to their business goals. They know that they no longer have the time needed to recover if they put their money on risky companies. If these companies go bankrupt, their lifetime financial goals with be severely affected.

Many of the middle class investors fall in this category. Even those who are not investing actively, usually give their money to investment managers who use this approach.

As you start your investment journey, you should aim to take this approach. Divide your funds according to your goals. If you have some extra funds, try your hand on picking short-term investment stocks. You only hold your short-term stocks for a week or two. You can sell these funds if you are satisfied with their appreciation.

However, do not just pick stocks mindlessly. Try to exercise diligence when you are picking stocks. Make sure that the company you choose to own has a strong business foundation.

Emotional investors

Most people fall into this category. They want to make their business grow, but they freak out every time something bad happens. Unfortunately, there is always an impending crisis in the financial world. The news is always full of negative information. If you are a nervous investor, these news will affect your decision making process.

Nervous investors tend to act based on emotion. When they hear negative news, they immediately want to pull their money out from the system. Unfortunately, most people have this kind of mentality when investing. Most of them do not have a plan on when to invest and when to pull their money out. As a result, they are more likely to do impulsive selling of their shares.

Even the ones with good plans laid out by their financial advisers tend to abandon their plan when they see bad things happening in the stock market.

There should be no room for nervous people in the stock market. Unfortunately, many people act based on fear in the market. The collective behavior of these people in the stock market creates major shifts in share prices. When they are hyped, they buy stocks. This pushes prices up. You should time selling your shares when there is hype in the market.

When the market is uncertain and news is full of gloomy information, nervous investors usually pull their money out prematurely. Again, the collective actions of people acting on fear create an impact in the market. The massive sell off of stocks, pulls the prices downward. This is a good time to buy.

Day Traders

Day traders make up the rest of the market. There are a lot them in the market. We do not call them investors because investing is not their goal. Instead, they are more focused on taking advantage of the short-term movements in the market prices.

Day traders have extremely short holding periods. In fact, most of them only hold stocks for a few hours. They look for stocks that may make tomorrow's headlines. They take the risk of buying shares of that company in bulk before the rest of the market catches on. They wait for the price of the shares of that company to rise as the company hits the news. When that happens, they sell their shares and make a profit.

Unlike real investors, day traders do not care about the track record or the performance of the company. Instead, they are more interested about the hype around certain companies. They take advantage of the gullible and emotional players.

While this method of participating in the stock market may seem exciting, it is usually very risky. Every time day traders buy stocks of new companies, they are taking massive risks with their money. Many beginners lose their entire investment funds because they fail to understand the risks of using this method in the stock market.

The Biggest Challenge of investing in the stock market

The biggest challenge when investing in the stock market is its sheer size. It is impossible for one person to learn about all the companies in the stock market. The number of companies in this market will overwhelm you. Because of this, experts like Warren Buffet suggest that people should only stay within their circle of competence.

You should also limit your choice of stocks to companies that you are knowledgeable with. Avoid buying the shares of companies that you know nothing about. You can start by choosing a sector in the market that you are already familiar with.

An insurance salesman for example, probably knows about all the insurance companies in the market today. If he starts investing in the stock market, it may be advantageous to start investing in companies in this industry first.

Major fluctuations can be scary for most risk adverse investors

Some investors cannot take the risks necessary to succeed when investing in the stock market. When they see that their investment is taking a beating, they become scared and they abandon their investment plans. You should avoid making this mistake.

When investing in the stock market, you should remember that the prices will always fluctuate because of the high activity of the market. Your goal when buying companies is to find the ones that are undervalued in the market.

Undervalued companies are the ones that are not reported yet in the media. They are usually silent performers whose value is yet to be seen by the market. The best investors research about these companies. They want to own shares of these types of companies early, when the demand for them are still low.

You will find that a company is undervalued by looking at its overall performance in its business operations. Companies with a solid business plan, with a great leader, and with great positioning in the market will eventually become a big player.

You want to own its shares before it becomes well known to the media. The biggest investing firms have a full department of people examining new companies and putting a value on their business. They check the viability of these smaller corporations and they try to see the potential for growth. If they feel like these companies have the potential to grow faster than the market, they will probably put money into it.

Investors are obsessed with company earnings

In the stock market, there is no other metric more important than a company's earnings. At the start of each quarter, competitive companies set their earning goals. A car company for instance, would set the number of units that they plan to sell in the following quarter. The same happens with other big companies in the stock market.

Publicly traded companies are obliged to pass an earnings report at the end of each quarter. This gives the investors an idea on how effective the company is in reaching its goals. It also allows the investors to see how well a company is performing compared to its competitors in the market. A company may deny that it is losing market share in the media, however, earning numbers will show if it is indeed true.

If all companies provide predictable earning reports, these reports would not have much impact in stock prices of companies. However, every now and then, there are surprises in these reports that cause the market to react.

Chapter 4 – The Bond Market

Bonds are an instrument used by businesses and governments to borrow money from investors. They are also sometimes referred to as debt instrument or fixed income investments.

They are called debt instruments because the bond issuers are basically just borrowers of money and the people buying bonds are the debtors. The bond acts like a contract that states the terms of the lender-borrower agreement.

Similar to borrowers, bond issuers also state the exact amount that they want to borrow. They also include the date of maturity of the debt. This information states a future date on which they will pay the entire debt to their investor.

The maturity period (time between the bonds were issued and their maturity date) is usually three or more years long. The contract includes the interest rate of the bonds. The interest, in this case, is the cost of borrowing money and it is the amount paid by the bond issuer to the investor.

The interest rate of the bond is also the reason why it is considered a fixed income investment vehicle. The interest rate of the bond declares its value. If a bond holder wants to sell his bond, he could do so as long as its price is below the total value of the bond. The total value of the bond is equivalent to the sum of the principal amount and the interest.

Risks of investing in Bonds

As with any type of investment, investing in bonds also has some risks. When companies and governments issue bonds, they intend to use the money for their own projects.

Governments do not necessarily need the money of investors to do projects. They just use taxes to fund them. They use this system to decrease the amount of cash in circulation. Because governments are not likely to go bankrupt, governments bonds are considered safe investments.

Big and small companies alike, also issue bonds to fund their growth. They use the money for business activities that increases the value of the company in the future. To be in the winning side of the bargain, the companies need to grow at a rate greater than the interest rate that they paid for the bonds.

However, unlike governments, companies could go bankrupt. When companies file for bankruptcy, they are no longer obligated to pay for debts. Because of this, corporate bonds are further classified based on their risks.

Bonds from big corporations are considered safer because the issuer is no likely to go out of business. When the corporation fails to meet their business goals, they could just liquidate some of their assets to pay off the bond holders when the bond matures.

Bonds from smaller companies on the other hand are riskier. These businesses do not have enough assets to pay off all their debtors. They also do not have a track record of success. This creates a sense of uncertainty in investors' minds. Because of the increased risk that comes with them, these types of bonds are often called Junk Bonds.

Interest rate – Risk Relationship

The interest rates of bonds are affected by its risks. If the bond is issued by the US government for instance, you could expect that they will pay the entire amount when the maturity date comes. The government will always have enough money to pay off its bonds. Because of the lower risk that comes with the bond, the interest rate of this type of bond is always lower compared to corporate bonds.

On the other end of the spectrum, Junk Bonds usually have significantly higher rates compared to government bonds. Junk Bonds are considered risky, making people reluctant to buy them. To encourage investors to take the risk, the issuers of Junk Bonds promise high interest rates. Investors for this type of bond expect bigger rewards for the risks they are taking.

The Bond Market

Sometimes, bond holders do not want to keep their bonds until the maturity date. Let's say you are a bondholder and you want to liquidate your bonds now. However, the maturity date is still five years from now. Your only option is to sell your bonds in the bond market.

Just like the stock market, bonds are also sold in their own market platform. Thousands of investors access this market to find investment opportunities. Just like stocks, assets in this market are bought and sold at their market price. The market price of bonds usually falls between the amount of the principal and the total value of the bond (principal invested amount + interest at the maturity date).

Many factors affect the prices of bonds in the market. It is also governed by the law of supply and demand. When the stock market is performing poorly for example, some investors from that market may want to protect a portion of their portfolio by investing a part of it in bonds. If many people are thinking of the same strategy, the demand in the bond market increases. This pushes the prices upward.

Aside from the law of supply and demand, the prices of bonds in the market are also affected by their respective maturity periods. Bonds that have longer maturity periods are priced lower than the ones with nearer maturity dates. The length of the maturity period affects the risk of investing in bonds.

By investing in a bond that will mature in 10 years, you need to keep your funds in the investment of that amount of time. You will not be able to use it for any other type of investment. By investing in bonds with longer maturity periods, you risk not being able to participate in other potentially big investment opportunities. Because of this, the bond's potential reward should be higher compared to the ones that mature in three years.

The goal of the investors in this case, is to buy lower priced bonds. After obtaining them, the investor has the option if they want to wait it out until the maturity date of the bond. When the bond matures, the investor gets the capital amount plus the interest promised by the issuer.

If the investor needs to sell his bonds, it will always be priced lower than the total value of the bond on its maturity date.

Why borrow money?

If businesses have the option to get more capital from the stock market, why would they borrow money and pay interest? The decision makers of these companies consider many factors when deciding on the best methods to gain funds.

While using equity does not require the company to pay money in the future, it also has its own downsides. Namely, the more owners a company has, the higher the risk that it will be taken over by the competition. A competing business for example, may buy enough shares in the company to become the majority shareholder. This strategy is called a 'hostile takeover'. By issuing bonds, companies prevent the growth of the number of investors.

While stock public offerings are often widely publicized, many frugal investors still prefer bonds over stocks. Bonds are treated as debt instruments. In time of the liquidation of assets of a company, the liabilities of the company are paid first before the shareholders. Bonds are paid first, even before preferred stockholders.

Chapter 5 – Investing in Commodities

The commodities market is another form of investing that can yield good rewards if you know what you are doing. Commodities refer to high-demand produce that are publicly traded.

The produce themselves are not traded in the commodities market. The investors and speculators in this market trade the contract for the future value of the product. Some investors simply call this as futures trading.

How does it work?

Let's take coffee for example. Coffee is a popular commodity because it is always in high-demand. Many countries produce coffee including countries in South America and South East Asia. John is a coffee expert and he decided to take part in the commodities trading of coffee.

On January 5, 2014, John went to the Brazilian Mercantile and Futures Exchange to make some deals. This place is one of the many exchanges where coffee futures contract is traded. He finds a seller of coffee and creates a futures contract with that person to buy 50,000 pounds of the commodity at $2/pound on January 5, 2017.

In the process, John's total capital should be $100,000 (50,000 pounds x $2/pound). However, he does not need to provide the money immediately after the creation of the contract. Instead, he only needs to put a portion of it in "margin account". For the sake of the example, let's say that John placed $50,000 in the margin account.

In this process, John does not actually buy 50,000 pounds of coffee and brings it home. Instead, John bought a contract to buy coffee in the future.

Because this type of commodity mostly comes from outside the US, many factors affect its prices. If coffee-plant specific virus attacked the plantations in South East Asia, for example, the supply of coffee in the US will be severely affected. The low supply would drive prices up.

If the price of coffee is higher than $2/pound by January 5, 2017, John makes some money. Let's say that the price of coffee at that time is $3/pound. The coffee that John bought in the past was sold for a total of $150,000 (50,000 pounds x $3/pound). John bought the future contract only for $100,000. With this particular deal, John made $50,000.

To illustrate a losing scenario, let's say that the supply of coffee on January 5, 2017 is abundant. Because of this, the price of coffee at the date is only $1.50/pound. The coffee that John bought for $100,000 was sold only for $75,000. However, John needs to fulfill his end of the contract. Because he vowed to pay $100,000, he needs to add another $50,000 in the margin account. He then sells the coffee he owns at the market price ($75,000).

In the losing scenario, John loses $100,000 and gains $75,000 for a net loss of $25,000.

Between the time the contract was created and its maturity date, the holder could trade it in the futures market. If the supply of coffee is running low for instance, many people may become interested in John's future contract. In the bonds and stock market, the traders and the investors dominate the action. In the commodities market, it is common for investors to sell their futures contract to actual buyers of their product.

Let's say the price of coffee peaked in the market at $4/pound by March. John obviously made the right call to bet on coffee. However, his contract is not matured yet. A lot of things could happen in the coffee industry in the following months before the maturity of his futures contract. To capitalize on the appreciation of the value of the commodity, John could tell his commodities broker to sell his contracts at the best price.

Many people would want to buy John's futures contract. People who actually use coffee in their business usually have representatives present in the Coffee exchanges. The companies that they represent want to find the best prices for the commodities that they need in the future. In this case, they want to ensure that they buy coffee at a fixed price.

The volatility in the market makes it difficult for businesses to calculate profit projections. By using contracts in the futures market, businesses that need coffee will be able to determine the exact amounts that they will need in the future.

This is a simple illustration of how futures contract in commodities could become an investment. However, real life commodities futures contracts are much more complicated than this.

Contract Options

One of the factors that make futures contracts complicated is the options added to it. For example, John's contract could include an 'extra-buy' option. This option gives John the privilege to buy more of the commodity at the given price between the date the contract was issued and the maturity date.

Multiple other types of options could be added to a futures contract. These options make it harder to put a price on a commodities futures contract.

While investing in futures is an opportunity to make your money grow, you should only participate in it if you know the industry of a certain commodity. You need to have insider knowledge on how the market in such commodities works and what factors commonly affect prices.

Chapter 6 – Investing in Foreign Exchange

In every securities market discussed above, there is always an asset being traded. In the case of the foreign exchange market, these assets are currencies of major countries. Just like in other markets, the law of supply and demand also governs the foreign currency market.

In the past, only central banks of governments and international banks made use of this market. However, with improvements in technology, it is now easier for everyday investors to start trading in forex.

Unique Market Characteristics

While other popular markets have a centralized place for trading, forex does not have one. Instead, a forex trader needs to transact with multiple dealers and financial centers to participate in the market. This also means that there is no organization or government that regulates the market.

Because most transactions are across borders of countries, traders could get away with insider trading. Insider trading refers to the use of privileged or exclusive information to gain money from securities trading. This technique in trading is illegal in the stock market.

Because the currency market has no governing body, there is no limit in the amount of investment that you can trade. The activity in forex trading revolves around the most popular currencies. This includes Yen, US Dollars, British Pounds, among others. There is always someone looking to buy or sell these commonly used currencies.

Foreign exchange investments are more liquid than other securities because of the large number of players in the market. The foreign currency market is probably the biggest open market in the world. The amount of daily transactions in this market is even bigger than the different US stock exchanges combined. Because there are so many people and institutions in the market, you will always find buyers for the currencies you are holding.

Unlike the stock and bond market, the forex market does not close on weekends and holidays. Because you are dealing with currencies from different countries, the trading action is open even at night.

Forex trading also has minimal extra charges compared to other types of investments. Because most forex brokers operate online, they have minimal maintenance fees for their business. They do not require management and clearing fees from their investors.

How Forex investment works:

When trading in forex, the investor always deals in pairs of currencies. The currencies used in forex markets are usually from developed countries.

Just like with other forms of investments, the goal is to buy low and sell high. You buy currencies by exchanging your native currency for a foreign one. When you sell, you exchange the foreign currency you are holding back to your native currency.

Let's say that your primary currency is the US dollar. You want to make money from the partnership of British Pounds and US dollars. At the time you exchanged your dollars to pounds, the exchange rate is $1.30 for each British Pound. An investment of $1,000 exchanges for 770 British pounds.

For your investment to grow, you want the dollar to weaken against the pounds. If the exchange rate rises to $1.40 per British Pound for example, your investment would have grown to $1,077 if you do decide to sell. In the process, you would have gained over $300 from just one point increase in the rates.

If the dollar becomes stronger in the length of time you are holding the British Pounds, you would have lost money from this transaction.

All the transactions add up to the money present in the banks. Because everything is done digitally, the foreign exchange brokers need to ensure that no money is created in their trading systems. It is up to the banks that the brokers are connected to regulate their activities.

Understanding currency pairs

Investors trade currency pairs in the Forex market. In the trading computer programs that are used provided by brokers, the currencies are represented by their three-letter acronym. The US dollar for instance is shown as USD while the Canadian dollar on the other hand is usually shown as CAD.

Here are some of the most popular currencies with their three-letter acronym:

US dollars – USD

Euro – EUR

Japanese Yen – JPY

British Pounds – GBP

Swiss Franc – CHF

Australian dollar – AUD

Canadian dollar – CAD

New Zealand dollar - NZD

The currency pairs are represented by two currencies separated by a forward slash (i.e. USD/CAD). The first currency in the currency pair is called the base while the second is called the quote currency. The resulting value reflects the amount of quote currency one needs to purchase one unit of the base currency.

Let's take the USD/CAD pair for example. You will need CAD$1.32 to buy a US dollar. Because of this we can say that USD/CAD=1.3200. The opposite currency quote should be

CAD/USD. This pair is equal to 0.76 because you need exactly 0.76 US dollar to buy one Canadian dollar at this exchange rate.

Let's say you have $100 USD and you want to buy Canadian dollars. In this case, you are interested in buying the CAD/USD currency pair. You will be asked to pay 0.76 for each Canadian dollar. At this rate, you will get around 132 Canadian dollars. For you to make money, you need to keep track of the value of the CAD/USD currency pair.

While there are hundreds of currencies in the world, only a few are valuable to investors. The casual investors only want to deal with commonly traded currencies to keep their investment relatively liquid. Among the hundreds of currencies in the world, here are the four most popular currency pairs for investors:

- EUR/USD

- USD/JPY

- USD/CHF

- GBP/USD

You will also find many retail dealers that trade these three less popular pairs:

- AUD/USD

- NXD/USD

- USD/CAD

These pairs and a few other less popular ones are the only currency pairs that are traded on a regular basis. To keep the liquidity of your money, you should keep your Forex trading activities within this scope.

Because of the limited number of actively traded currency pairs, it is easier to keep track of your forex investments than it is to keep track of companies in the stock market.

Forex Investing insights

When investing in foreign exchange, you need to learn the different factors that affect the value of the currency you invested in. The top most traded currency pairs are usually from developed free markets. Investors usually avoid currencies of companies like China and Russia because of the heavy governments influence in their value.

China for instance, chose to devalue their currency to boost exports in recent years. The purposeful devaluing of currencies makes it difficult for people to speculate. Furthermore, people with insider knowledge of scheduled devaluing in the future could take advantage of the situation. Try to avoid participating in currencies whose values could be manipulated by their government.

Now that you know the currencies to avoid, let's discuss the factors that affect the value of currencies around the world:

1. Economic activities in the country of origin

Some trading gurus suggest that buying a country's currency could be likened to buying shares of the country. You could expect the currency of a country to rise in value if the overall value of the country also increases. Among the many metrics used to put a value on countries, the change in the Gross Domestic Product or GDP is probably the most commonly used.

The GDP is the total value (in US dollars) of products and services created within the economic borders of the country. The change in the GDP is usually expressed as a percentage. If the GDP grows, it signifies that the country is going in the right direction in terms of the government's economic policies.

Having a big increase in GDP has a long and short term effects. In the long term, the currency is expected to increase in value. If one of the currencies in the pair you are trading improves its corresponding GDP significantly, the news may increase the value of that country's currency.

In the short term however, the GDP change may result in a decrease in the value of the currency. High GDP means that the country is self-sustaining. If the GDP growth comes with low inflation and high trade deficit, this may mean that the product and services is not coming out of the country of origin.

2. Trade balance

When you are invested in a county's currency, you should keep track of reports about their trading output to foreign countries.

To make the currency stronger, the country needs to improve the value that it exports. If a country is exporting a lot of goods and services, other countries will need more of that country's currency. This increases the demand for the currency and it increases the value of that currency.

3. Interest rate

Changes in the interest rates have a direct relationship with the value of the country's currency. If the interest rates of a currency increase, the value of the currency also increases. This happens because of the actions of global investments funds. They want to buy more of the country's currency to get more profits. The increased demand for the currency also increases its value in the Forex Market.

4. Economic stability and growth

Signs that show economic stability and growth have a long term impact on the value of a currency. Political stability for instance, creates a good image for the country of origin. The countries with the most active currencies listed above have good track records for peaceful transitions of power. This makes their currency relatively safer than others in the market.

If there are signs of instability however, this will have a negative impact on the value of the currency. Political instability can result to inconsistent economic policies. This in turn will lead to a possible decrease in the GDP, higher unemployment and high inflation rates.

Aside from the politics of a country, the rate of unemployment may also have a negative effect on the currency of the market. When there is a high rate of unemployment, the country is using up resources for the large number of unproductive people. The inefficiency of the country creates a negative image for its currency. This leads to a decrease in value of that country's currency.

5. Central bank initiatives

The central bank is in control of everything that relates to the country's currency. For example, they could decrease interest rates to boost the borrowing in the economy. In turn, this also leads to a decrease in the demand for that particular currency, decreasing its market value.

Aside from the interest rates, the central bank also controls the amount of physical money in the circulation. If the supply of money is uncontrolled inside a country, it may lead to inflation. It is up to the Central Bank to control the flow of cash in the economy.

They are always in a balancing act between catalyzing growth and controlling the budget and debt deficit. If they do their part properly in partnership with the central government, the country will show promising improvement and avoid the threats of recession and economic crashes.

However, if the central bank neglects its duties, it may lead to an economic crisis. If the debt crisis of a country goes out of hand for instance, it may lead to a big depression in the market. This will also decrease the value of the currency of the country.

6. Natural calamities

A country's ability to survive natural calamities also has a short term effect on the value of its currency. Because of the size of the US for example, it has the ability to withstand most natural calamities. Even if a strong hurricane hits the east coast for instance, it will only affect a small part of the country. The country and its economy will continue to keep going. The effects on the country's currency are temporary.

In contrast, countries like Japan and Switzerland are small. They are commonly visited by typhoons and earthquakes. When these natural calamities happen, the entire country is affected. There may be a halt in the productivity of the economy. If the natural calamity has devastating effects, it could also stall the industry and general effectiveness of the industries in the country. These events may have short term effects on the value of the currencies of these countries.

Knowing when to buy and sell

Your role as an investor is to keep track of the factors that affect the currencies that you own. Let's say you have a dollar fund with $100,000 and you decided to keep track of the JPY/USD pair. Because you are planning to buy their currency, you need to time your entry to the market when your target currency is priced low.

You should take advantage if any of the factors stated above affect the value of the Japan Yen in relation to the US dollar. You could also buy when the US dollar is particularly strong. When these two factors align, you may enter the market by buying the JPY/USD pair. This will ensure that you buy the foreign currency at a low price.

When buying currency, the general value of each currency is of little value to you. You are more concerned with the relationship of one currency to another. In our example, your focus should be on the individual factors affecting the value of Japanese Yen in relation to the performance of the US dollar.

If both currencies are performing well for instance, you may see very little change in their exchange rate. However, if the Japanese Yen is performing well while the dollar is falling, the currency may be too expensive for you at that moment.

To check the past relationship of the currency pairs, you should consult charts of past prices. This will give you an idea if the currency pair has a stable and predictable relationship. A simple Google search will give you access to these charts.

Let's say that the Japanese Yen is valued at $0.0085. You will be able to buy a total of 11,705,500.00 JPY.

After buying, you should keep track of the events happening in both Japan and the US. In particular, you need to keep track about the news affecting their economies. You could go back to the list above to see the economic factors that affect the value of currencies.

As of the moment, you have 11,705,500.00 JPY. As political and economic situations change, the dollar equivalent of this amount will also change. These changes bring about daily fluctuations in the value of the USD/JPY pair. Keep track of it and try to find the best time to exchange your Yen back to USD.

Most people who start with forex trading think that it is easier than trading stocks because of the low number of functional currencies that you need to keep track of. Do not underestimate the market.

While there are only a few factors that you need to keep track of, the high rate of fluctuations in this market may surprise you. Because of the many players and the lack of a central governing body, Forex prices   fluctuate much more than stocks and bonds. The volatility of the market serves day traders well. If you don't plant to actively keep track of the market, this is not the type of investment for you.

Chapter 7 – The Real Estate Market

While real estate is not a type of security, it is still an important aspect of the investing industry. The types of investments discussed in the previous chapters were all intangible forms of investments. Investing in real estate differs from them because you actually need to buy a property to take part in the market.

However, it is important to keep your eyes open for good real estate investments as a way to diversify your assets. When people make money from their portfolio investments, they usually try to obtain real properties as a way to protect their money from the volatility of the market.

While the real estate market could also be volatile, your real properties will not vanish overnight like the market value of your bonds or stocks. As long as you keep them as your properties, you will be able to earn certain types of income from them.

Types of income from real estate

There are three general types of incomes that you can get from your real estate investment. When hunting for real properties, you should consider the types of income that they could bring you.

Production income

Production is the primary use of real estate properties. In fact, Adam Smith, considered the father of modern economics, referred to all units of production with the term 'land'. Production income refers to the profits that you can make by working the land.

The most basic form of production income is probably farming the land to make money out of its produce. This requires active labor and constant improvements in farming techniques. The amount you earn from it depends on the type and quality of your produce. Even if you don't like this way of earning money, it may be the best option if the land you own is located in a rural area.

While farming could be a lucrative business, it is not considered by many as a passive way of earning money.

Because farm lands are relatively cheaper than urban properties, you will easily find properties that already have the facilities needed for production. A piece of land for example, may already have a line of apple trees planted in it and you only have to modernize the cultivation and the harvesting of fruits to make profits.

Rent your property

Rent is the second way of earning from real properties without the need to let go of it. You could rent the entire place (like with residential housing) or portions of it (like hotels and apartment buildings).

Most people owning land in the city rent it to the highest paying renters. If you own a building in a prime spot for instance, it may be more profitable to rent the space out to business owners. You will need to find a business owner whose business fits perfectly with the spot.

On the other hand, if the building is located among high-end residential areas, you may earn more if you rent it out to the neighborhood's target market.

When people talk about rent, they mostly focus on residential spaces. However, renting to other business-minded individuals should also be an option. Farmland owners for instance, may not have the time to manage and operate their farms. To monetize the land, they may rent it to other farmers in the area.

Areas around a property could also be rented out for advertising. A building owner for instance, could rent the side of his building to a business owner. The managers of the business could put up their own ads for a monthly fee.

Sale (Value appreciation)

Aside from renting, you could also earn through property development. You may have heard stories of businessmen, the likes of Donald Trump, transform a small piece of land to a giant tower. Corporations also transform hectares of land to create suburban residential areas near major cities.

While you may not be able to do the same projects because of lack of resources, you may do something similar on a much smaller scale. If you have a knack for home design, you could buy an undervalued property, make improvements in it and sell it for a profit.

There is only profit in this business activity if you can buy low and sell high. In other markets, the value of the investment appreciates if the market value increases. The same goes for real property investments. However, the appreciation of this type of investment is more within the control of the property owner.

A developer for instance, could build houses in a piece of land to increase its value. A house flipper could make a neglected home more livable and make a profit from his efforts.

To earn from this kind of business, you should have the capital to buy the property and pay contractors for renovations. Also, you need to learn the marketing skills of selling houses.

Types of properties

To succeed in a real estate business, you need to specialize in managing only one type of property. If you just focus on buying residential lots with the intention of renting them, you could create a system that will make business operations more efficient. This will minimize costs while maintaining your income. You will also be able to gauge the true value of the properties when buying them. Having this knowledge allows you to buy properties at lower prices.

Production properties

As stated above, these types of properties are used for creating products and services. The income from which depends on the value of the product or service produced.

Farms and rural properties are converted into production properties because there isn't a lot of demand for the property. While this type of property is generally cheaper, most of them have low potential for capital appreciation and income opportunities.

Residential properties

This type of property is meant for housing purposes. The size and the location of the property usually determine the price of the rent and the overall value of the property.

People looking for residential property to buy or to rent are also mindful of the details of the structure. The integrity of the foundation of the home is always one of the primary concerns. Aside from this, small damages in the structure that need to be fixed could be a cause for lowering of sales prices.

While residential properties tend to be more expensive than their rural counterparts, they also appreciate faster. As cities develop outwards, developers buy suburban properties to build malls, business districts, schools and other social areas. If a developer builds one of these types of properties near your area, the value of your residential property instantly increases.

Vertical residential properties

Aside from the usual single home residential properties, you could also invest in vertical residential properties. Condominiums are a common example of this type of property. They are bought and sold by units. By buying a unit, you become the owner of everything inside it.

In the case of condominium buildings, you also become a part owner of the rest of the building. The home owners association in these building becomes the governing body of the entire property. They uphold the rules and regulations in the use of the shared parts of the property. They also make sure that certain privileges that make the property valuable are maintained. This includes maintaining the integrity of the building and hiring the right people to maintain the shared areas.

Vertical properties are popular among cities where space is limited. Certain neighborhoods in New York only have this kind of property. Vertical properties also populate the skyline of overly populated cities like Tokyo.

Business rental properties

As stated earlier in the chapter, business owners need prime spots to reach their customers. If you own a property in such a location, you could earn by renting it out to businesses.

While you could find short term renters, businesses often operate through leases. A lease is similar to renting. However, in a lease, the renter and the property owner agree on a specified period for leasing. The lease period usually spans at least a couple of years.

The lease could also include an agreement of an increase in the lease prices at the end of the renting period if the business owner chooses to renew the contract.

Leasing to businesses poses a new set of advantages and disadvantages. The general advantage is that the property owner ensures that occupancy of the business space he rents out. It ensures a guaranteed income for the duration of the lease.

However, depending on the length of the lease, the property owner could be at a disadvantage. Longer leases keeps the property income potential limited. If the rent around the area increases, you will not be able to reap the benefits because you should follow the terms in the lease contract.

Avoid taking long leases. Keep lease contract as short as possible, especially if there is a high demand for the property.

Making the process easier

Now that you know how to make money through real properties, you could already start investing in one that is within your budget. When you do decide to invest in real estate, you need to make the process of making money from them easy. It could only be a true investment if you do not need to put too much of your productive time in making income.

To do this, start by listing down the types of services that you need to make the property work. If you plan to rent properties, you will need a property manager. When you start out, you will only have one or two properties. You don't need a manager for this. However, as you roll your capital, the number of properties you manage will increase. It will be more difficult to manage each one. If this happens, get a property manager to do the basic management tasks for you.

You will also need certain types of repair professionals to help fix things around your property. Find a reasonably priced worker that provides good quality of work. As the number of properties you own increase, the frequency of fixes also increases. Eventually, you may need to hire a full-time or part-time employee to do these fixes.

If you plan to start buying and selling properties, you need to connect with passionate and active brokers. Look for one that specializes on the income-bracket that you serve and the area where you operate. Most of them could be found in brokerage firms around your city. To find out how much you should pay them, set up an interview. They will tell you the specific details of their services.

When talking to brokers, avoid signing exclusive listings with them. This way, you could have multiple people listing your properties. Only allow exclusive listing agreements if you believe that the real estate broker could do better than all other brokers combined.

Chapter 8 – Managed Investment Funds

In the previous chapters, we discussed the common types of investment securities. You need to study those markets before you could effectively participate in them. If you start investing without preparing for it first, you may end up losing money in these markets.

Most people however, do not have the patience, time or the resources to learn expert advice on how to invest actively in these markets. Because of this, most people opt to join investment funds.

Investment funds are designed to let casual investors to participate in the market, even if they do not have a lot of knowledge about the matter. They are run by government agencies or investment companies. In the case of the latter, the management takes a small percentage of the investment every year as payment for managing their portfolio.

Mutual funds

Mutual funds are probably the most popular form of managed funds. Mutual funds are companies that gather money from investors and add them to their investment funds. The gathered funds are then, invested in various types of securities. A mutual fund company usually states the type of fund they are running. They also state the goal of the fund and the investment strategies they use to achieve their goals.

Advantages of joining mutual funds

- You do not have to keep track of the market

You do not have to spend your time inspecting the market every day for buying and selling signals when you invested in mutual funds. Instead, you only need to put your attention on the market when you are about to sell off your stocks.

Mutual funds generally discourage short-term investments by imposing penalties for investments that are too short. This prevents massive sell-offs of mutual fund shares. If you want to buy and sell shares, this is not the best investment vehicle for you.

- You can start right away

Mutual funds make it easy to start investing. Some of them even partner with big banks so that you can just do your transactions within the banks where you store your money. To start with mutual funds, you only have to fill out the forms to declare your identity, provide some proof of identification and money to buy shares from the mutual fund company.

- Investment process can be automated

Mutual funds also make it easy for some people to save their money. Most people have difficulty saving money. They just do not have enough discipline to stick to their financial goals.

Mutual fund companies sometimes partner with banks to set up automated investments. The company could automatically subtract money from your bank account and allocate them to your preferred funds. Because the money is automatically deducted from your savings account, you never get a chance to spend it. If you think that you will have trouble saving money because of old habits, setting up an account like this one is probably the best option.

- Easy access to different types of security investments

If you want to invest directly to the different types of securities (i.e. stocks and bonds), you need to learn how each market works. You will need to learn the different factors that affect the market. Most importantly, you will need to study the data available from each company you plan to buy stocks of bond from.

Mutual funds allow you to invest with the only basic knowledge in these markets. You no longer need to pick stocks. You only have to decide when to buy and when to sell your mutual fund shares.

One mutual fund company could have multiple funds. Each one could be invested in a different type of security. You don't have to leave your mutual fund company if you want to transfer your assets from one type of security to another.

Fund Management

Each fund has its own fund manager. In actively managed funds, the manager is responsible for allocating the fund assets to various securities. If the fund is invested in the stock market for example, the fund manager actively picks the stocks and chooses the timing of buying and selling. His goal is to outperform the market where his funds are invested.

Types of Mutual Funds

Each fund has an underlying asset where it will invest its assets. Based on this information, mutual funds could be one of the following types:

Equity funds

Equity mutual funds are funds that invest their assets solely in the stock market. These types of funds are actively traded. Because the prices of stocks in the stock market are always fluctuating, equity funds are usually considered high risk investments. Mutual fund companies only allow aggressive investors to invest in their equity funds.

Equity funds also have higher potential rewards compared to funds invested in fixed income investments. In a booming market, investors who bought their shares low will likely see their portfolio size grow faster than other types of funds. However, when the market is down, this type of fund is also the most heavily affected.

Bond funds

Bond funds are more conservative in terms of its potential for growth. However, it also has lower risks compared to equity funds. As the name suggests, these types of funds are solely invested in the bonds market. This type of fund tries to avoid the volatility of the market and protects the investors' money from the big drops commonly seen in the stock market.

An investor participating in bond funds should expect moderate growth when the market is booming and also moderate losses when the general market is down. Compared to equity funds, its average returns could be less than half during bullish markets.

When the market is down on the other hand, the negative impact in bond funds are generally lesser compared to the losses of equity funds.

Balanced funds

The balanced fund was created for people who want to enjoy the fast growth of equity funds and the fund protection properties of bond funds. Balanced funds try to find the perfect allocation between the two. Assets in this type of fund are invested in both markets.

The fund manager will be able to transfer the majority of the assets to the stock market when he anticipates that the market will grow. He could then transfer most of the fund back to the bonds market when the stock market is doing poorly to protect the assets of the fund.

While in theory, some people would expect that this type of fund will outperform both funds. In reality, it does not. Balanced funds' average returns are usually just in between the returns of the bond funds and equity funds.

Special mutual funds

Mutual fund is also classified according to the unique markets it could participate in. For example, some companies have an 'emerging markets' equity fund. This type of market is still an equity fund. However, it is only invested in the stock market of emerging markets or small economies.

Some types of fund also invest in specific international economies. If you think that European countries will do well in the next few years, you could invest in Euro equity funds.

Some funds are also classified according to their operating currency. In the US for example, people earning in pounds could avoid foreign currency risks by investing in pound denominated mutual funds.

Criticism of mutual funds

Mutual funds are essential in the market because they allow even beginner investors to participate in the growth of the economy. However, the privately owned mutual funds are run by business entities. Just like any other type of business, mutual fund companies just want to make money. They want to be paid for their efforts in managing people's investments.

To pay for their day-to-day expenses, these funds ask for management fees. These fees are used to pay for the cost of running the business. Some of the expenses covered by the management fee include payment to the fund manager and his employees. It is also used to pay for utility bills of their offices as well as salary of their customer support employees.

While it is fair for the mutual fund companies to ask for a payment for their services, some of them ask too much. The management fees are taken from the total value of the fund. It is usually stated as a percentage of the fund value. This fee is taken annually.

Critics of mutual funds that are run by corporations point out that these companies also take money even when the fund is losing money. This means that on top of your investment losses, the fund will still deduct its management fee from your investment.

Most importantly, other investors like Warren Buffet and Ray Dalio point out that actively managed mutual funds usually perform worse than the market that they participate in. They argue that the high management fees take its toll in the value of the investment of the investors.

Two types of mutual fund fees

To start investing in mutual funds, you first need to choose a company. When you are inspecting different companies, take note of the fee that the mutual fund company requires.

The first type of mutual fees is called sales load. Sales loads are usually the amount paid to the mutual fund solicitor who facilitates your investment. These people are paid on a commission basis. Most mutual funds companies have two types of sales loads, front-end and back-end loads. You will be asked to choose between the two every time you buy shares from the mutual fund company.

Front end sales load are deducted from your account the moment you deposit your investment. Let's say the front-end sales load of the mutual fund company is 1%. You invested $100,000 and chose this type of load. $99,000 of your invested amount will be used to buy mutual fund shares while $1,000 will be deducted for the front end sales load. You already lost 1% of your money the moment you started investing.

The second type of sales loads is called back-end sales load. This is the opposite of the front end sales load, in that, it is subtracted when you sell your shares in the fund and liquidate all your assets.

Back-end sales load rates are usually bigger in the first year. Most mutual funds reward long term investors by decreasing the sales load every year that the investor keeps his money in the mutual fund.

To illustrate, let's say you invested $100,000 when you started and you chose the back-end load option. Your fund has a 2.5% back-end sales load and it deducts by 0.5% every year. The entire amount you invested will be used to buy shares.

Before your first anniversary, your invested amount grew to $105,000. If you chose to withdraw your money within the first year, you will need to pay 2.5% of the amount you withdrew. In this case, $2,625 will be deducted from your funds.

Let's say that you didn't withdraw and in the second year, your funds grew to $110,000. However, by the second year, the system deducts 0.5% from your back-end load. If you chose to withdraw the entire amount from the fund within the second year, 2% or $2,200 dollars will be deducted from your withdrawn amount.

The back-end load rate will become smaller the longer you keep your assets in the mutual fund. In our example, your fund will be free of sales load deductions by the end if your 5th year of keeping your assets in the company.

Avoiding sales load entirely

Some companies do not charge sales loads to their investors to give investors the freedom to buy and sell mutual fund shares as they see fit. If possible, you should start with these types of mutual funds because you will have a better chance to make your portfolio grow with them.

Mutual fund solicitors know that having sales load turns customers away. Most of them would not even talk about the fees of their company in their presentations. To find out about their sales loads, ask them directly about it when they are presenting their products. By asking them a direct question, they will be forced to tell you the truth. Avoid investing in mutual fund companies where the solicitors don't tell you about the fees.

Aside from sales loads, companies also impose a management fee on their funds. The management fee collected by the fund from its total invested assets is supposed to be used for the maintenance of the company. This includes payment of the salary of employees. It is also used for the expenses involved in investing such as fees paid to the brokers of different security markets. This is also where the company takes its profits.

One of the downsides of investing in mutual funds is that the management fee is subtracted from the total assets in management regardless of the fund performance.

If your company subtracts 1% in management fee for example, the mutual fund company will keep subtracting that amount every year even though it did not make your money grow.

While all mutual fund companies have management fees, the rate of the fee varies from one company to another. Actively managed funds tend to have higher fees. These are funds where in the fund manager picks the securities to buy and times the buying and selling of assets.

Generally, funds that are passively invested have lower management fees because they don't have to pay a hotshot fund manager to pick stocks and time buying and selling of assets. These types of funds have rules on how their assets are invested. The allocation of the assets is predetermined by these rules. They have scheduled adjustments to make sure that the allocation follows the rules.

Top investors and financial gurus recommend most beginners in investing to find no-load funds with low management fees to start investing. You can find these types of funds in index funds and other passively invested mutual funds. You still need to check the fees from third party sources though, to ensure that they really have low fees.

Tax sheltered retirement funds

People living in the US are discouraged by most personal finance gurus to start investing in the stock market or other investment markets immediately. They argue that the investors are better off putting their money in their retirement funds first. Because these types of funds are tax sheltered, your funds will grow faster than regular mutual funds. The only downside is that this type of funds has limits. They could be maxed out if you put in enough contributions. Ideally, you should max them out before investing anywhere else.

Investing in Index funds

Index funds are a type of passively managed mutual fund. While regular mutual funds are managed by a fund manager, the allocation of assets in an index fund is automated. The computers that manage the index fund are programmed to adjust the allocation of the assets regularly. The goal of these programs is to mirror a specific index in the market.

An S&P 500 index fund for example, aims to base its allocation of its assets on the capitalization of the companies in the S&P 500 index. If Apple Inc. for example has a weight of 3.1% in the S&P 500 index, the computer program will allocate 3.1% of the investable assets of the fund to that company. It will continue to allocate funds based on the weight of each company in the index.

As a result, the performance of index funds closely mirrors the performance of their respective index. This is enough to beat most of the actively managed funds in the market.

Index funds are gaining popularity because they are generally cheaper to maintain. Some index funds could charge as low as 0.2% in management fees.

The performance of index funds is also more predictable than managed funds. While most managed funds promise to beat the performance of the market, they rarely ever do. Popular investing personalities like Warren Buffet and Tony Robbins recommend their followers to use low-cost index funds.

Chapter 9 – Investment Strategies

When you invest in the investment vehicles discussed in the previous chapters, you should follow an investment strategy that fits your goals. The principles that follow will ensure that you do not take too many risks and you put your assets in the best position to grow.

Buy low and sell high

In all your investing endeavors, the goal is always to buy assets at the lowest price. When buying securities, the prices of assets depend on market conditions. The varying supply and demand for these assets will make their prices fluctuate.

However there are times when all asset prices are down in a particular market. In times of economic uncertainty for example, active investors and day traders try to avoid the stocks because there are no short-term profits to be gained. The general investing public also does the same because of the negative news about the market.

This is usually a good time to buy stocks if you have cash available for investing. You could choose between buying discounted stocks of companies due to bad market conditions and joining load-free and low management fee mutual funds. Either way, you will get good prices because stock prices are down across the board.

When investing in bonds and other debt instruments, the prices of newly issued bonds depend greatly in the interest rates imposed by the Central Bank. When the government is trying to boost business activities in the country, it will lower interest rates for borrowing. Because the cost of borrowing is low, businesses are more likely to issue bonds of their own to investors.

This increases the value of bonds bought and sold in the bonds market. Prices go up because the newly issued bonds have low interest rates.

The Central Bank also increases the interest rates from time to time to lessen the impact of unpaid debt in the economy. This prevents the budget (from taxes) and debt deficit from becoming too big.

When the Central Bank increases the interest rates, people and businesses generally avoid borrowing because of its high cost. However, this drives investors to the newly issued bonds in the market because these assets have better profits.

Because investors want the newly issued bonds, fewer investors go to buy bonds with the lower interest rates. This decreases the demand and the prices for these types of bonds in the market. This may be an opportunity to buy low. You may find some bonds sellers that already want to liquidate their asset. Because of the lower demand for these bonds, you could get them at prices nearer to the principal investment.

Aim to become an expert in your chosen market

You will only become an expert in putting a value on assets if you specialize in investing only in a few markets. If you invest in too many markets, you will not have enough time to keep track of important events affecting the markets. Most financial experts suggest that you focus first on putting money in low-cost managed funds like index funds. These funds set your investing in autopilot. You only need to focus on the best time to buy and sell.

If you have more time on your hands, you could take the opportunity to learn investing in one of the markets discussed in the previous chapters. Most people start with the stock market because it is the easiest market to understand. Compared to other types of markets, there are many resources about investing in stocks because it is a popular topic.

When studying stocks, you should set an investing strategy that fits well with your level of risk aversion and your personal financial goals. If you do not like big losses, you could stick with stocks of giant blue chip companies that give out dividends often. However, you should also know that the value of these stocks have lesser potential for growth because these companies are already big.

Smaller companies have bigger potential for growth. However, the risk for these companies to become bankrupt is higher because of their lower market capitalization.

Most of the time, your choices for companies to buy will be limited by the prices per share of these companies. If you only have $10,000 to invest, investing in companies whose stocks cost $1,000 per share is not an option. You are better off starting with companies that have lower prices so that you can diversify the distribution of your assets.

As stated in the previous chapters, you should also specialize in the market sectors that you want to invest in. Ideally, you should start with well-established sectors. Most people for example, are excited to invest in tech companies because of their potential for growth. However, this sector is fairly new to the market. It is also more difficult to put a value on companies in this market because a lot of them have no tangible products.

Unless you have many connections in this industry, avoid taking part in this sector for now. Instead, start with sectors that you are involved with. Doctors for instance, know more about pharmaceutical companies than they do tech companies. They can make use of their knowledge in the industry to make informed decisions.

You should do the same. Start with sectors that you are genuinely interested in. This will lessen the learning curve for investing and will give you a better chance to succeed.

Learn about financial safe havens

After learning to invest in the stock market, you could choose another market to take part it. Smart investors transfer their money to safe havens when the market is down. A financial safe haven is an investment instrument less likely to be affected by the market negatively. You put your money in it to avoid losses in more volatile investment instruments. Ideally, it should at least be able to beat inflation so that your funds still keep its spending power.

Among the many investment instruments, gold is probably the most popular safe havens. Big investors tend to transfer their money to gold during tough economic times. As a result, gold prices tend to climb when markets like stocks and bonds are performing poorly. Gold, however, is not the only safe haven in the market. Treasury bills and other money market instruments are also in high demand in bearish markets. However, most investors prefer gold because of the extremely low interest rates of Government treasury bills.

In recent years, investors have been considering funds from other countries and continents as safe havens. After the 2008 real estate crisis for instance, some big investors transferred their money to funds invested in South East Asia. These markets performed well right after the recession in the US. Many investors who took this route made profits from this safe haven.

While financial safe havens are meant to save you from losses, they are also subject to market risks. When choosing to transfer your funds, choose according to the needs of the situation.

Invest actively

If you have a large sum of money to begin with, you could start investing actively in your chosen market. To succeed using this strategy, you need to become an expert in certain industries. You should focus on these industries when investing so that you have a better chance of making good, informed decisions.

When using this strategy in the stock market for example, an investor reads up on all the news regarding the companies he is interested in. He also inspects the financial statements of the company. He checks whether the company's profit is consistently growing. Aside from this, most investors also make sure that the companies they are eying are led by people with integrity.

Aside from becoming an expert in your chosen market, you should also be aware of global economic events. Because the US is the biggest economy in the world, it has a stake in the economic situation of other countries. Any event that affects the mood of investors, also affect the US stock market.

Being the largest economy and market capitalization in the world, the US stock exchange also invites the biggest crowd of day traders. Day traders control trillions of dollars in assets in the stock market. These traders are usually very aggressive in their investment strategies. They enter the market with big investments when there is hype in the market and they exit fast. They want to earn money fast so they sell immediately when they make profit.

Thousands of day traders enter and exit the market every day. However, when the economy is down, they all avoid the stock market like a plague. Instead, they transfer their money in less affected markets like gold. The massive pull-out of traders from the market causes a chain reaction that causes the market to fluctuate.

If you want to be an active trader, you need to anticipate the collective movements of these investors and traders in the market. They usually follow the hype while avoiding the losses when the hype ends. Instead of following their lead, you should instead do due diligence when researching about the companies you invest in.

Only invest if you are sure that the company will last long. If you buy only strong companies, the assets you invest have a higher chance of surviving even if the market crashes tomorrow. You will not fear losing your investment because you know that the company will still be there when the market rebounds.

It also helps if you take classes in investing if you want to become a good investor. Even if you don't have the funds to take classes right now, you could start with massive open online courses or MOOC. You could take personal finance and economic classes free from these websites. You could proceed to more specialized courses if you have the funds to take them.

Consider cost averaging if you cannot invest actively

Cost averaging (also called dollar cost averaging) is the method of investing the same amount of money regularly. Let's say you invested in an equity mutual fund. However, your job prevents you from keeping track of the market all the time. Because of this, you cannot make informed decisions on when to buy stocks.

Cost averaging allows you to continue investing without the need to track the market all the time. Let's say you could only afford to invest $50 every month. Every month, you invest $50 to your mutual funds without considering the current market condition.

This strategy is the remedy for people who have no discipline in investing actively. It takes away the thinking part of investing. Because the market is on an uptrend most of the time, people are more likely to see positive results with this strategy in the long run. However, this strategy does not work if you have been investing in a market with inflated values for a long period.

If you started investing in the US stock market in 2004 for example, you would have felt the full impact of the 2008 economic crisis if you used this strategy. While cost averaging has its disadvantages, it is still better than putting large sum of money in savings account where its value will continue to decrease because of inflation.

Focus on your goals when you invest

Many people start investing without a purpose behind it. They put their money in the market, not knowing what to do with it if it actually grows. This is the reason why most people fail in the market. They don't know what they want to accomplish in the first place.

If you want to succeed in your investments, you should have a financial goal in mind. You should then, create a system that will make it easier to save and invest for your goal.

For your investments to reach your target amounts, you need to consider three important factors, length of your investment, amount of your capital, and the average rate of return of your investment vehicle.

The length of investment, generally, has direct proportional effect in your investment. The longer you keep your money in the market, the higher your potential return will be because of compounding interests. Let's say you invested $100,000 in the stock market and you managed to make your money grow to $108,000 by the end of the year.

If you keep your money invested in the market the following year, both your initial capital and the returns of your investments will be used for new investment opportunities. They will be subject to the rate of growth of your investment on the following year. If you manage to grow your investments by 5% in the second year, your investment will grow by $5,400 instead of just $5,000.

Over the years, compounding interest will continue to make your investment fund grow exponentially. However, you need to keep your money invested for this to take effect. This also exposes your funds to market risks longer. Big market dives like recessions will have a big impact on your investment. However, if you stick by the best practices in investing, you will have a better chance to regain the value that you lost as the market rebounds.

Aside from the length of your investment, the rate of return of your investment also affects the growth of your funds. When actively investing, you should choose the investment vehicles that have the highest potential for growth. When investing in stocks for example, you should focus on companies that are more likely to increase in value. The trick is to invest in them before the rest of the market finds out about it.

Investing in the stock market gives you one of the best opportunities to grow your fund. However, it also has one of the biggest risks of losses. This kind of balance between risks and rewards is present in all investment opportunities.

Chapter 10 – How to Start Investing

Now that you have a general idea of what investment opportunities are available, let's discuss how you can get started. In this chapter, we will discuss how you can invest in some of the common investment vehicles discussed above.

General way of starting to invest

Investing in securities is easy. First you need to find a person or company that will introduce you to the market. Companies that provide advanced investment advice generally cost more in fees. They may also require larger investment sizes.

However, you could cut costs by sticking to Do-It-Yourself companies. These companies do not provide premium services. They only provide you with the platform that you can use to buy and sell securities. There is such a company for each type of security discussed in this book.

While their services may be limited, they usually provide a knowledgebase in their website for people who want to learn on their own. This type of system is common among online Forex trading services. Some may even provide you with play money to practice your stock-picking skills.

You can access the databases and tutorials of these companies by depositing an initial investment to their service. The amount required for the initial investment varies. For Forex, it could be as low as $100. However, the premium companies require a much higher amount.

When joining these online brokers, make sure that you practice due diligence when researching about these companies. Make sure that these companies are legitimate and are registered to operate within the US.

You should also read reviews about them to make sure that you are not entrusting your money to scam artists.

Investing in managed funds

Managed funds like mutual funds are probably the easiest investment tool to start with. While the requirements vary depending on the investment company, they usually require minimal paperwork.

To start, you need to go to the office of the company you have chosen in your area. While most of these companies have online services to hasten the process, the process is easier for beginners if they have someone to talk to.

They will ask you to answer questions regarding your ability to tolerate financial risks. If you want to invest in high-reward investment types like equity funds or index funds, you should avoid answering conservatively to their questions.

Aside from your risk tolerance, the mutual fund company may also ask you questions regarding the source of your funds. This is a standard practice among financial institutions to prevent money laundering.

In general, your investment fund size should correlate with your current financial status and your source of income. If you are unemployed with no past work experience, the mutual fund company may question your source of funds. In some cases, mutual fund companies decline applications from people with questionable character and sources of funds. This prevents criminals from using the investment system to launder their money.

If the mutual fund company finds no issues with your application, they will give you a form for buying mutual fund shares. In this form, you need to place the type of fund that you want to invest in. If there is a sales load for the purchase, you also need to specify that in this form. Most importantly, you will need to specify the amount of money that you will invest in the fund.

After application, it may take at least half a day for the mutual fund company to process all the information. By the following day, the company should be able to confirm your purchase of shares.

In your part, you should take note of the price per share and the number of shares you bought. If you are going to invest multiple times in the future, you should keep a record of it in a spreadsheet or a ledger. You should also keep all your investment receipts in one place. Put them in a place that you can easily locate when you need to liquidate your funds.

Investing in tax-sheltered mutual funds

State regulated retirement funds are usually the best type of investment vehicle to start with because they are not taxed. The value of this type of fund is likely to grow fast. If you work for a good company, your employer may also match your contribution to your retirement fund. This increases the growth of your fund even faster.

If you are not yet invested in your 401(k), inquire about it with the person responsible for the compensation and benefits tasks in your human resources department. They should be aware of the best way to make your 401(k) grow.

Max your tax-sheltered retirement funds first before you invest in regular investment funds like private mutual fund companies.

Investing directly in stocks

If you want to have direct involvement in to stocks and bonds, you will need to have a representative in the market. You will need to look for a brokerage company and open an account with them. The process is similar to investing in mutual funds, however, brokerage companies tend to have higher initial deposits than mutual funds. Before you go to the brokerage firm, call them up first to know their initial deposit requirement.

In the case of stocks, you will see two types of brokerage firms. The first group is called full-service brokerage firms. This type of brokerage firm advertises to give you all the support you need. Some of them may even provide you with a broker that you can call anytime for your investing questions.

While their services are great, they also only cater big clients. On average, the minimum initial deposit for these types of firms is around $60,000. You may not be ready for that kind of investment.

Discount brokerage firms cater to people who are not yet ready for big financial commitments with their brokerage firms. On average, this type of investment firm usually requires around $1,000 for their minimum initial deposit. While the initial deposit is lower, these types of investment firms also have very limited services. They will just give you support in buying and selling stocks. They rarely have customer support services. You should expect to do all the research on your own.

Online brokerages are also becoming popular nowadays. Unlike the other two types above, these types of brokerage firms only have few customer support offices. Instead, they encourage clients to only transact online and through the phone. You will need to pass all your requirements by mail, email or fax.

Investing in Real Estate

To start investing in real estate, you will need to prepare your funds. Ideally real estate investments should be funded with the use of cash. If you use financing to fund your investment, you may have trouble making profits from it.

Also, choose the time when you enter the market. Check first if there is an economic bubble in the market. You will know if there is one if the prices of real estate properties are rapidly rising. The market will eventually correct itself and the bubble will burst, decreasing the value of all real estate properties across the board.

If you are sure that there is no bubble, you could start looking for a real estate broker in your area. You will need to let them know of your goals for the property. They will look into the market for properties that match your goal.

Look for a specialized broker by checking their listings. Brokers usually have a website where they put their listings. If you plan to flip houses for instance, you need to look for a broker who specializes in listing low-priced residential housing.

When you do find a broker that fits your standards, build a relationship with them so that you will know first if they have good properties to offer.

When buying, the sellers may try to bump you over your budget. Because of this, give a low initial offer to your broker. The broker will deliver the message to the seller regardless of how low the price is. In most cases, you will be able to find a halfway point with the sellers.

When renovating homes, be mindful of your budget. The sooner you finish the project, the sooner you will sell it. Make sure there are no delays in your project timeline.

After selling your property, contact your broker again to buy a new one. The cycle continues to make your portfolio fund grow.

Conclusion

Thank you again for downloading this book!

Investing can be scary in the beginning. As you learn through experience, you will be able to develop the confidence to take comfortable levels of risk. While most people are spending their money on the things they will barely remember, you are saving for the future and letting your money grow.

Your money will grow if you use a strategy that fits your personal goals and you stick to a sustainable investing system. Now that you have a general knowledge of the investment markets, find opportunities to gain experience in the real world. Start saving your capital and put them in your preferred investment vehicle.

Keep learning about the investment type that you have chosen and build your portfolio without taking unnecessary risks.

Thank you and good luck!